WELCOME TO THE WORLD OF ANIMALS

Rabbits and Hares

Diane Swanson

Gareth Stevens Publishing
A WORLD ALMANAC EDUCATION GROUP COMPANY

Please visit our web site at: www.garethstevens.com
For a free color catalog describing Gareth Stevens Publishing's list of high-quality books
and multimedia programs, call 1-800-542-2595 (USA) or 1-800-387-3178 (Canada).
Gareth Stevens Publishing's fax: (414) 332-3567.

The publishers acknowledge the support of the Canada Council for the Arts and the Cultural Services Branch of the Government of British Columbia in making this publication possible.

Library of Congress Cataloging-in-Publication Data

Swanson, Diane, 1944-
    [Welcome to the world of rabbits and hares]
    Rabbits and hares / by Diane Swanson. — North American ed.
        p. cm. — (Welcome to the world of animals)
    Includes index.
    Summary: Describes the physical characteristics, behavior, and habitat of rabbits and hares,
some of which can run at speeds of forty-five miles per hour or more.
    ISBN 0-8368-3316-3 (lib. bdg.)
    1. Rabbits—Juvenile literature.   2. Hares—Juvenile literature.   [1. Rabbits.   2. Hares.]
    I. Title.
    QL737.L32S92   2002
    599.32--dc21
                                                                            2002021105

This edition first published in 2002 by
Gareth Stevens Publishing
A World Almanac Education Group Company
330 West Olive Street, Suite 100
Milwaukee, WI 53212 USA

This U.S. edition © 2002 by Gareth Stevens, Inc. Original edition © 2000 by Diane Swanson.
First published in 2000 by Whitecap Books, Vancouver. Additional end matter © 2002
by Gareth Stevens, Inc.

Cover photograph: Victoria Hurst/First Light
Photo credits: Tim Christie 4; Robert Lankinen/First Light 6; Thomas Kitchin/First Light 8;
Helen Longest-Saccone/Marty Saccone 10; Brian Milne/First Light 12; Jerry Kobalenko/First Light 14,
20, 30; Peter McLeod/First Light 16; C. Swift/First Light 18; Darwin Wiggett/First Light 22, 24;
Victoria Hurst/First Light 26, Lynn M. Stone 28

Series editor: Patricia Lantier
Design: Katherine A. Goedheer
Cover design: Renee M. Bach

Printed in the United States of America

1 2 3 4 5 6 7 8 9 06 05 04 03 02

599.32
S

Contents

World of Difference

It's hard to tell rabbits from hares — unless you happen to spot their newborns. Rabbits start life without any fur, while hares arrive in fluffy coats.

As adults, hares — which include jackrabbits — are usually larger than rabbits. Hares also have longer back legs and feet. In fact, the snowshoe hare was named for its big back feet. Like real snowshoes, they are long and wide, making it easy to move across snow. In winter, extra hair grows on the feet, which also helps keep the snowshoe hare from sinking.

People sometimes confuse rabbits and

Many snowshoe hares are brown in summer, white in winter, and mixed in fall and spring.

The marsh rabbit has short ears — for a bunny — but it hears just fine.

hares with rodents, such as mice, rats, porcupines, and beavers. All these animals have long, sharp front teeth, built for gnawing. But rabbits and hares have an extra pair of sharp teeth that grows behind the front teeth in their upper jaw.

Rabbits and hares are well known for having long ears and short tails, but they

A TALE OF A TAIL

Many countries have stories about a hare's short tail. Here's one from Ireland:

Long ago, an old man asked a long-tailed hare for directions through the woods. "Follow me," said the hare. "I'll show you the way."

As the man hurried along, he tripped and fell into a pit. "Grab onto my long tail," said the hare, then it pulled hard. The old man leaped out of the pit, but the hare's long tail snapped off, leaving just a stump.

don't all have them. For instance, volcano rabbits have short ears and no tails.

Worldwide, there are more than forty different kinds of rabbits and hares. About twenty kinds live in North America, including the European hare and European rabbit that people moved from their original homes.

The smallest rabbit or hare is the pygmy rabbit, which weighs only as much as a grapefruit. The biggest — the European and arctic hares — can weigh sixteen times more than a pygmy rabbit.

Where in the World

You can find rabbits and hares almost any-place. Some kinds live close to seashores; others, on hillsides and tall mountains. Some make their homes in city parks and gardens; others live in the windswept Arctic. From dry deserts to soggy swamps and from grasslands to forests, rabbits and hares can be seen nearly everywhere.

Hares usually live in open spaces. They rest in forms — shallow pits or holes that they dig in the soil. Sometimes they hide out in hollow logs or in little tunnels dug by other animals.

North American rabbits often live in

A hare snuggles down beneath some low-growing branches.

In a warm coastal forest, an eastern cottontail is taking life easy.

sheltered spaces, such as woods. Like hares, most rabbits rest in forms, but European rabbits use burrows. They make a large maze of burrows — called a warren — which they might use for several generations. If the ground isn't suited for digging a lot of warrens, European rabbits might fight to keep others from taking over their homes.

Warm Up, Cool Down

Thick fur helps protect rabbits and hares from the cold. But fur isn't always enough. In icy weather, arctic hares huddle close to the ground and tuck in their ears and tails. They might also tunnel into snowbanks.

In hot deserts, black-tailed jackrabbits can't sweat to keep cool. They release body heat through blood vessels in their long, thin ears. On sizzling days, they might dig or enlarge a small burrow, then take shelter in its shade.

Pilots of low-flying planes can spot trails where many black-tailed jackrabbits live. These hares usually follow the same paths to their favorite feeding places. They pack down the soil and plants as they go.

Hares and rabbits are found throughout many countries, including Canada, the United States, and Mexico. Some kinds live in many places; others, in very few. The volcano rabbit, for example, lives only on mountain slopes in central Mexico.

World Full of Food

Most rabbits and hares find food in the dark. Evenings and nights are safer times for them to be out. Through the summer, they graze on plants such as grass, clover, and bushes. They also eat garden vegetables in cities and on farms. In winter, when there's not as much food around, many rabbits and hares feed on dried plants, twigs, and bark. Snowshoe and arctic hares even eat meat now and then, if they find the body of a dead animal, such as a fox.

The big front teeth of rabbits and hares are strong and sharp enough to gnaw hard food. They have a tough coating to protect

Mmm, good! Many kinds of rabbits and hares feed in lush fields of grass.

13

A herd of arctic hares lunches on Ellesmere Island in northern Canada. They often live in small groups.

them, and they never stop growing. As rabbits and hares gnaw, they tuck flaps of skin behind their front teeth. That helps the animals avoid swallowing any dirt or slivers. A split top lip allows them to stuff plenty of food into their mouths. It also makes their noses wiggle when they eat.

Frozen Dinners

Winter snows often bury arctic willows — short, bushy plants that the arctic hare eats. It sniffs around until it smells the willows under the snow. Then it digs down to reach them, using the sharp, curved claws on all four feet.

If the snow is crusted with ice, the arctic hare might try to pound holes with its feet. If that doesn't work, it can gnaw through the crust with its front teeth. They stick out farther than the front teeth of most other hares.

Many rabbits and hares feed alone, but some kinds, such as antelope rabbits, eat in groups of up to one hundred. All kinds gobble their food fast, then head for safe, quiet places.

Rabbits and hares produce soft, moist pellets of partly digested food. They eat these pellets the minute they come out of the animals' rear ends, then digest them all again. That's how rabbits and hares get more nutrients out of their food. The waste their bodies cannot use forms hard, dry pellets.

World of Words

Thump. Thump. Thumpety-thump. When they're afraid, rabbits and hares might stomp their back legs hard enough for others to feel the ground quiver. That's a warning — something's definitely not right!

Rabbits and hares that live near one another sometimes see warnings, too. When European rabbits and black-tailed jackrabbits run from danger, the white fur on their tails sends a signal to others.

Waste pellets can be used for another kind of "talking." Some males use their own pellets to mark out territories. Then they

A jackrabbit tears away. Its tail is raised like a white flag, warning nearby hares of danger.

search for mates inside the area. The smell of the pellets is a sign that tells other males to keep out. Male European rabbits sometimes stack up pellets to mark their burrows. They might also rub their burrows — and some of the female rabbits — with a special oil from their chins. The smell from that oil says, "Mine. All mine."

A cottontail can sniff out a message left by another rabbit.

HERE'S TO HARES AND RABBITS!

These furry critters are amazing. Here are a few reasons why:

- **In bursts, black-tailed and white-tailed jackrabbits can race at speeds of 45 miles (70 kilometers) an hour or more.**

- **The teeth of a cottontail rabbit can grow 4 inches (10 centimeters) in a year.**

- **Rabbits can produce a lot of heat. One man housed hundreds of them in a greenhouse — to help warm his plants.**

A rabbit or hare doesn't often use its voice. But if the animal is grabbed, it can make a high-pitched squeal or shriek. The crying might encourage other predators to compete for the rabbit or hare. That can give the captured animal a chance to escape.

Sometimes rabbits and hares use low growls and gruff grunts to say, "Go away." A soft clicking might mean, "I'm nervous." And as a mother is feeding her young ones, her gentle purring says, "All's well."

World of Senses

Sniff, look, and listen. Being able to sense danger in time to hide or escape can save the lives of many rabbits and hares. So it's lucky for them that they smell, see, and hear as well as they do. Day and night, they put all these sharp senses to good use.

The big, bright eyes of rabbits and hares take in almost everything that's around them. Set on either side of the head, these eyes can see an enemy coming from any direction — even from behind. As soon as a rabbit or hare spots danger, it freezes. Not so much as a flicker from its watchful eyes gives its position away.

Who's there? An arctic hare uses its nose, eyes, and ears to detect enemies.

Rabbits and hares are always twitching their noses, checking the air for smells. As they open their nostrils wide, they draw all the scents deep inside. Their noses have about 100 million sensors each, all working to pick up different scents. That's more than six times the number of smell sensors in your nose.

Taking a bath is easy for a rabbit. Its wet tongue makes a handy washcloth.

WASH AND DUST

Hares can have bad hair days — and so can rabbits. But they usually take very good care of their coats. They wash themselves by licking whatever their tongues can reach. Then they wet their paws and use them to scrub other parts, such as their cheeks.

Hares and rabbits might also treat themselves to dust baths. The dry soil helps prevent their fur from getting too oily. It also relieves itches caused by insect pests.

Rabbits and hares have a keen sense of hearing, too. Without moving their heads at all, they can turn their ears to pick up sounds. They catch faint and distant noises.

To locate danger, jackrabbits seem to depend more on their hearing than they do on their sight. At the first hint of any danger, they stand their long ears straight up. Then they twist them this way and that until they discover the source of the sound.

Dangerous World

Gray or brown coats help rabbits and hares hide. The animals blend in well with soil, rocks, and dry grass. In late fall, some grow thick white coats that match the color of snow and ice.

Many predators hunt for rabbits and hares, including lynx, foxes, weasels, wolverines, hawks, owls, eagles, and snakes. When chased, European rabbits might duck inside a warren. They have more than one opening for popping in and out.

Rabbits and hares often try to outrace danger. They bound away, springing off their back legs and feet. Their lightweight

Even though an earth-colored cottontail is hard to spot on the dirt, it will be lucky to live a year.

Speeding away, a
snowshoe hare tries
to escape an enemy.

bodies help make jumping easy, but
rabbits and hares have several different
running styles. In a single leap, a racing
snowshoe hare can cover a distance the
length of two beds placed end to end.
A black-tailed jackrabbit may jump
especially high every four or five leaps,
so it can take a good look around.

GAME OVER

A European hare is grazing in a field. Less than 150 feet (45 meters) away steps a fox. The hare looks straight at the fox and rises up on its back legs. It makes itself easy to see. But why?

A fox rarely chases its food. It tries to creep close, then hides until prey comes near. If a hare stands tall, the fox knows it's been spotted. There's no point trying to catch the speedy hare, so the fox usually looks for different prey.

Some rabbits and hares confuse their predators by hopping from side to side and circling around as they race. They usually try to avoid water, but they can swim if they have to. The slower-moving marsh rabbit seems almost comfortable in water. It can float with only its eyes and nose poking out.

If it is caught, a rabbit or hare might pretend to be dead. Predators don't always eat their catch right away, which can give their prey a chance to escape.

New World

Most rabbits and hares have big families. Some females have up to twelve young at once, and they might give birth three or four times a year.

Rabbits are born in nests that their mothers make. A European rabbit uses grass to line a special nesting chamber inside her burrow. Most other rabbits in North America dig shallow holes among tall grass or bushes. They line these holes with leaves, grass, moss, and soft fur that they pull from their own bodies.

Newborn rabbits are helpless. They have no fur, and their eyes are shut tight.

Young rabbits snuggle together in a comfy nest of straw and fur.

This mother can feed her whole hungry family at once.

Before their mother leaves the nest to eat, she covers her young with a layer of nest lining. It hides them and helps keep them warm. When the mother returns, she feeds them her rich milk. The rabbits grow fast and move out of the nest after about three weeks.

Young hares are lively right from birth. They have furry coats to keep them warm, and their eyes are wide open. Within a few hours, they're able to hop around.

Like most North American rabbits, hares are born above ground. Arctic hares must wait until the snow melts to make a simple nest on the ground, often in moss. Mother hares usually visit their young only once a day to feed them milk. In three to four weeks, the hares are ready to leave their mothers and — if they must — to race away from predators.

Hopping Right To It

At birth, cottontail rabbits may be no longer than your thumb. But they grow fast. They can double their size and triple their weight in just two weeks! Then they start crawling out of their nest and hopping around. Sometimes they play by jumping right over one another.

As they start to graze grasses, young cottontails move farther from home. But if their mother senses danger and stamps her feet, they freeze or run for cover.

Glossary

burrows — (n) holes in the ground made by animals for homes or shelter.

digest — to change food in the stomach and intestines so it can be used in all parts of the body.

flicker — (n) a sudden quick movement.

gnawing — biting at or chewing on something and wearing it away with the teeth.

maze — a network of paths, such as a tunnel that has many passages.

pellets — the small, round waste produced by rabbits and hares.

predators — animals that hunt and eat other animals.

sensors — parts of the body that respond to tastes, smells, sounds, light, or other stimulation.

territories — the grounds, or areas, where animals live or search for food and mates. Animals defend their territories from others.

warren — an area of ground filled with many burrows, where rabbits live.

Index